Fruits and Gifts of the Spirit

Fruits and Gifts of the Spirit

Thomas Keating

Lantern Books
A Division of Booklight Inc.

2000
Lantern Books
One Union Square West, Suite 201
New York, NY 10003

© St. Benedict's Monastery, Snowmass, CO 2000

Printed in the United States of America

Library of Congress Cataloging-in-Publication Data

Keating, Thomas
Fruits and gifts of the Spirit / Thomas Keating.
    p. cm.
ISBN 1-930051-21-2 (alk. paper)
1. Spiritual life—Catholic Church. 2. Fruit of the Spirit.
3. Holy Spirit. I. Title

BX2350.2.K426 2000
234'.13—dc21

00-062995

Thanks to Bonnie Shimizu and Reverend Robert Dunbar for their editorial assistance.

CONTENTS

—1—
THE DIVINE INDWELLING

FOR MOST PEOPLE, ORDINARY LIFE IS characterized by the sense that God is absent. Yet, a little metaphysics would alert us to the fact that, if God were not present at every moment, we would not be here either. Creation is not a one-time event. It is God's ongoing gift on every level from the humblest quark to the highest stage of consciousness.

St. Teresa of Avila wrote: "All difficulties in prayer can be traced to one cause: praying as if God were absent." This is the conviction that we bring with us from early childhood and apply to everyday life and to our lives in general. It gets stronger as we grow up, unless we are touched by the Gospel and begin the spiritual journey. This journey is a process of dismantling the monumental illusion that God is distant or absent. When our particular petitions are not answered, we become even more convinced that God is absent. This is an irrational position, however, one based on the judgment of emotion, not reason. Unfortunately our unruly emotions do not obey reason and will; they have their own dynamic. Whenever our reason and will decide to do something, our emotions get into a huddle and decide whether or not they will go along with them. If our plan contradicts their perception of what is pleasant or unpleasant, we have a riot on our hands.

The start, middle, and end of the spiritual journey is the conviction that God is always present. As we progress in this journey, we perceive God's presence more and more. As we emerge from childhood into full, reflective self-consciousness, our concept of how God is present in us is usually vague and primitive. The spiritual journey is a gradual process of enlarging our emotional, mental, and physical relationship with the divine reality that is present in us but not ordinarily accessible to our emotions or concepts.

The dogma of the Trinity is presented to us as one God in three divine persons. The first person is called Father.

The second person is called the Word. The third person is called the Holy Spirit, which means breath. Did you ever know a person who was a word or a person, who was a breath? That we do not should alert us to the fact that, when we speak of God, we are not talking about any person we know.

The concept of persons in God refers to relationships that are only analogies of relationships in human affairs. Hence, we must not expect God to be present in the way other people are present. The chief fruit of Old Testament spirituality was a long-term education that gradually weaned the Chosen People away from their narrow concept of God as one among many other Near Eastern gods to the Transcendent One. The monotheistic God is the great gift of Israel to humanity.

God is present to us all the time but inaccessible as long as we have preconceived ideas and judgments based solely on the feedback our senses and feelings provide. Jesus' sayings might be paraphrased: "The reign of God is close at hand—not distant or absent. It is within you and among you."[1]

Thus, the fundamental theological principle of the spiritual journey is the Divine Indwelling. The Trinity is present within us as the source of our being on every level. Each level of life from the most physical to the most spiritual is sustained by the divine presence. To go to liturgy or to prayer thinking that God is absent prevents us from properly relating to the divine presence.

The reign of God is basically what God does in us. The divine is present as energy sustaining our physical, mental, and spiritual activities without a moment's interruption. Jesus is calling us to full human development, re-rooting us in our source, and enabling us to experience that this divine energy is infinitely tender, compassionate, nurturing, enabling, and empowering. Jesus' experience of the Father was Abba, God of infinite concern and tenderness for every living thing, especially human beings. His experience of God was revolutionary in the religious context of his day. His understanding is reflected in the commentaries of the Fathers of the Church, and now needs to be made the first lesson in every catechetical instruction and constantly repeated in sermons and homilies. The Divine Indwelling of the Holy Trinity is a truth of faith that is easily forgotten or avoided. Yet it is the one on which a radical personal conversion depends.

In our Christian tradition we believe the Word of God, revealed in scripture, is addressed to us. That Word also became flesh in order that Jesus' example would give us a blueprint of how to become fully human and fully divine. The eternal Word of God addresses us through scripture and the liturgy to awaken us to his abiding presence within us. Contemplative prayer is our opening and awakening to this relationship, to what God is doing for us, has done, and will do.

Scripture for the early Christians was not so much read as listened to, because the Christians did not have books. If you only heard the Gospel once a week and were interested in the spiritual journey, you would go to church all ears and listen to the readings with the whole of your being. We have been so desensitized by reading everything under the sun that the aliveness of sacred scripture does not easily come through. We must convince ourselves that there is a special presence of Christ in scripture that speaks to the hearts of those who are open and prepared. The Holy Spirit nudges us to perceive that what we hear refers to our personal situation and is meant to be a challenge and an encouragement to us. Once we understand that the Gospel addresses a presence within us that already exists, listening to the word of God becomes a process of gradual enlightenment.

The Divine Indwelling Unfolds in Prayer and Action
The early Fathers of the Church called this process the development of the spiritual senses. The external senses perceive the immediacy of material reality. The spiritual

senses perceive the immediacy of the divine reality in various forms by means of a gradual process in which the Word of God is assimilated, interiorized, and understood. As the process advances, the Fruits of the Spirit enumerated by Paul (Gal. 5:22–23) and by Jesus in the Beatitudes (Matt. 5:3–11) begin to emerge. These are signs that we are waking up to the divine presence.

The first stage of this process is listening with the undivided attention of one who wants to learn from a great teacher. In the Christian scheme of things, Jesus is the enlightened one who lives in the Christian assembly as the glorified Christ.

The liturgy juxtaposes texts to awaken us through words and symbols to the divine presence within us, and how it operates in our lives in both prayer and action. Prayer, the sacraments, and good works are all directed toward one purpose: to awaken us to whom we actually are, but do not yet know. The reception of the Eucharist is not a passing visit from Christ, but an awakening to his abiding presence within us, leading us into the further experience of the Father.

The Spirit bears witness to Christ's resurrection by empowering us with the Fruits of the Spirit and the Beatitudes. On the literal level, all we can do is listen to the message with good will and begin the process of dismantling our illusion that God is absent. In daily life the action of the Spirit increases as we try to put the values of the Gospel into effect. The monastics of the Middle Ages called this the moral level of scripture. When we are moved by the beauty and example of Jesus' life, we take courage that it might be possible to overcome our emotional programs for happiness that prevent us from accessing the full light of God's presence and action within us.

When the Word of God addresses us at a deeper level, we move to the allegorical understanding of scripture. We become aware that the same graces that we are hearing about in the Gospel are taking place in our personal lives. If Jesus could put up with the faults of the Apostles, he might put up with ours. At the allegorical level, one begins to understand the deeper meaning of scripture to which Jesus invited his disciples when he said, "If you have ears to hear, please hear," implying that they were not listening at the level at which he was addressing them. The Word of God is not only addressed to our ears, to our minds, and to our hearts; it is addressed above all to who we are at the deepest level. We are rooted in God, and by accessing that divine energy we are united with God and able to do what Jesus did: be a manifestation of God's tenderness and compassion among the people we serve and love.

The allegorical level awakens us to the fact that Jesus is inviting us into the commitment of friendship. This commitment opens up the various levels of union that the Fathers of the Church called the unitive way. The unitive way is the awareness of the abiding presence of God, a presence that is not undermined by what we feel or think, by what others do, or even by tremendous tragedy. We have found our Source. We become the Word of God and express the divine presence, just as Jesus expressed it in his daily life.

Each time we move through faith to a new level of hearing the Word of God, all our relationships change: to ourselves, to God, to other people, and to the cosmos. Then we need to spend considerable time integrating all our relationships into this new perspective.

As we read the scripture in an attitude of listening and respond to it with openness, reflection, and love, we interiorize and assimilate the message. In addition, scripture moves us to respond to the good things that we read about. Thus, prayer becomes the spontaneous response to the presence of the Word of God. This Word is not only present as a sound, but as a person. When we speak of the Word of God, we mean both the written word of God and the Word of God enfleshed in Jesus. Both words are knocking at the door of our inmost being where, because of our weak faith, Christ seems asleep, so to speak. Since we have never or only rarely experienced his presence, we assume that he is absent. As faith grows, that illusion is gradually diminished and overcome.

The spiritual journey is often presented as the purification of illusion, liberation from seeking the wrong things or too much of the good things, and freedom from the compulsions that arise from the misguided search for happiness that is still present in our unconscious and manifests itself in upsetting emotions. The afflictive emotions arise when something we do not want happens, or when something we do want does not happen. Our decision to follow Christ on the conscious level is not enough to heal the wounds of original sin. The unconscious programs for happiness that we bring with us from early childhood, and which we are not fully aware of until we vigorously pursue the spiritual journey, continue to upset us when they do not achieve their desired objects.

Thus, if power or control is our predominant program for happiness, we can make all the resolutions we want not to be upset by circumstances that are out of our control—and still the feelings of anger, grief, or discouragement arise when something we planned is frustrated. We are always struggling with what we want to do or decide to do and with the feelings that oppose our good resolutions. This is the area that we must address in daily life. The sense of the radiant energy that Christ communicates when his word has finally resounded at the deepest level within us begins to work its way into all our thinking and activity in order to enhance our capacity to respond with the kind of love that motivated him.

The spiritual journey, then, teaches us the following:

1. To believe in the Divine Indwelling within us, fully present and energizing every level of our being.
2. To recognize that this energy is benign, healing, and transforming.
3. To open to its gradual unfolding, step by step, both in prayer and action.

Our prayer, as contemplative persons, is the constant exercise of faith, hope, and charity (Divine Love), and takes place in the silence of our hearts as we listen to the Word of God—not just with our ears or minds, but with our inmost being. God speaks best by silence. This does not mean that we do not have unwanted thoughts during prayer, but that we return again and again to the basic consent of self-surrender and trust. We say "yes" to that presence, and every now and again enter into union with it as we identify the divine presence in Christ's humanity with the divine presence within us. When we say, "Come, Lord Jesus," we should remember that Christ is already here and that his coming means that he becomes more and more present to our consciousness. He does not move. We move. This process is one of consent to God's presence, of surrender to it, and of transformation into it. As we learn to listen to the Word of God within us, we develop greater sensitivity to the Seven Gifts of the Spirit, allowing the divine energy to manifest itself appropriately during prayer and in the events of daily life. Jesus comes to us in the Eucharist to be with us all the time and to suggest how we can lead our human lives in a divine way.

---

1. Luke 17:21. The Greek word *entos* means both "within" and "among."

—2—
THE FRUITS OF THE SPIRIT

THE FRUITS OF THE SPIRIT ARE INDICATIONS of God's presence at work in us in varying degrees and forms. Through the Fruits, the Spirit is becoming a reality in our lives. By manifesting the fruits in daily life we bear witness to the resurrection of Christ in a most profound manner. It is not so much preaching or teaching, but our rootedness in the Spirit that communicates Christ's life to the people around us—to our family, friends, and those with whom we work. If we are rooted in the Spirit, these fruits inevitably begin to appear.

I often use the example of the spiral staircase as a symbol of the purification that gradually takes place through contemplative prayer. In doing this I mean to suggest that every time we move to a new level of recognition of our weakness and dependence on God for everything, we experience a kind of inner resurrection. To put it in terms of the Twelve Steps of Alcoholics Anonymous, the more we realize how "unmanageable" our lives are—how helpless we are to practice the virtues and to imitate Jesus—the more life becomes an adventure in allowing the Spirit to move us and to accompany us in daily life.

Our temperament type, our number on the enneagram, and all the other things we can find out about ourselves through self-help programs are useful. Still, the main thing we need to know about ourselves is that we are unable to do any spiritual work under our own power. We are totally dependent on the Divine Spirit.

The Spirit is present to our inmost being all the time, inviting us to let go of our self-centered projects and to allow the Spirit to be the source of our actions at every level. With that kind of trustful dependence on the Spirit, each time we accept a new sense of our own weakness and lack of virtue there follows an inner resurrection. This is manifested by the experience of the Fruits of the Spirit.

The Fruits are the first indication of our transformation in Christ. As we descend the spiral staircase into the depths of our own being and into the center of our nothingness, the Seven Gifts of the Spirit, which are even more mature fruits, begin to manifest themselves.

Centering Prayer is a method to become more and more sensitive to the Spirit within us.

The Spirit is present within us by virtue of our Baptism, when we were anointed with the Spirit. Unfortunately, when we are not available to the Spirit, we think that the Spirit is absent. The power of the Spirit is intensified in the sacrament of Confirmation, when the Seven Gifts of the Spirit are explicitly transmitted to us. Our unconscious contains all the emotional trauma of a lifetime (that we have repressed) as well as enormous levels of energy and creativity. Every significant event of our life history is recorded in our bodies and nervous system. The undigested emotional material of a lifetime must be moved out in order for the free flow of grace and the natural and spiritual energies in the unconscious to manifest themselves. These energies appear as the qualities of charity, joy, peace, kindness, generosity, faithfulness, gentleness, and self-control.

The Fruits of the Spirit are nine aspects of the mind of Christ. They are listed by St. Paul in Galatians 5:22–23.

They activate and bring to maturity the graces of Baptism and Confirmation. They are the direct opposite of the bitter fruits of the false self—also listed in Galatians 5:19–21: promiscuity, licentiousness, enmity, contention, jealousy, quarreling, factionalism, and envy. The Fruits of the Spirit grow together with the theological virtues of Faith, Hope, and Charity. The Beatitudes are the ripe fruits of that transformation.

The first Fruit of the Spirit is *Charity* or, in the Greek, Agape, which means self-giving love as opposed to self-seeking love. Most of us know love as desiring something or someone. This is the kind of love the Greeks called Eros, a powerful and necessary kind of love but one that is meant to grow into the self-giving love that the Gospel calls charity. Charity is not almsgiving. It is rather a participation in God's unconditional love.

As a result we witness our former habitual attitudes unwind and begin to love people whom we normally despise or can't stand. Faith in God's presence in others enables us to overlook personality or character defects that cause us difficulty. We can begin to accept them, and perhaps someday we may be able to welcome them. The growth of charity leads to self-surrender to God and to the compassionate love of others. The quality of Christ's love is the source of its vitality; the continual tender and loving awareness of the presence of God is its reward.

The second commandment of Jesus is to love our neighbor as ourselves, and it is rooted in the recognition and acceptance by faith that the Divine Presence dwells in every human being. Perhaps there is someone at home or at work whom we would like to stay as far away from as possible. The first thing that attracts us to those with whom we have difficulties is the fact that God is present in them; we place our faith that God is there. Our efforts to accept people are based on a truth that we can't immediately see or feel, but that we believe. Accepting the movement of the Spirit enables the life of the Spirit to go on increasing in us.

Jesus has given us a new commandment and that is "to love one another as I have loved you" (John 14:34). This way of loving is much more demanding. It is not simply a movement of faith in the abstract. It is accepting each other in our individualities, in our opinionatedness, in the things that drive us up the wall, in what seems physically or emotionally repulsive in other people. We accept people just as they are because Christ has accepted us just as we are—with our lengthy list of limitations, faults, sins, and hang-ups. God's unconditional love poured forth in our hearts by the Holy Spirit goes on showing love, no matter what happens and even in the face of opposition and persecution.

Where does this charity come from? It is being infused into us in the silent seedbed of contemplative prayer. The whole of contemporary society is contrary to that movement. In daily life we meet with the endless projects of people with false selves similar to our own who are seeking symbols in the culture or in their environment of survival and security, power and control, affection and esteem. These people manifest their over-identification with their ethnic, family, religious, and national group. Their attitudes are confining and limiting, whereas the movement of the Spirit leads to freedom.

The second Fruit of the Spirit is *Joy.* Joy is an abiding sense of well-being based on the experience of a conscious relationship with God. It is the sign of liberation from the false self and the growing awareness of the true self. Flowing from joy comes the freedom to accept the present moment and its content without trying to change it. Bliss might be described as the fullness of joy. It is the abiding sense of being loved by God and of being permanently established in his presence. It is the experience of the living water that flows from the divine Source in our inmost being, which Jesus spoke about in John's Gospel:

"If anyone thirsts, let him come to me and drink. Out of that person's inmost being will flow rivers of living water." John the Evangelist adds: "This he spoke of the Spirit who would be given to those who believe in him" (John 7:37–39).

The third Fruit of the Spirit is *Peace*. Peace is the pervasive sense of contentment that comes from being rooted in God while being fully aware of one's own nothingness. It is a state that endures beyond the ups and downs of life, beyond the emotions of joy and sorrow. At the deepest level one knows that all is well, that everything is just right despite all appearances to the contrary. At all times one can pray with Jesus, "Father, into your hands I commend my spirit" (Luke 23:46).

The fourth Fruit of the Spirit is *Meekness* (kindness). Meekness is freedom from the energy of hostility, hatred, or outbursts of anger. Anger is necessary for human health and growth. But it needs to be transmuted into a growing capacity to persevere in the pursuit of the difficult good, especially the immense goods of the spiritual journey and of the imitation of Christ. The growth of meekness opens us to the continual awareness of God's presence and the acceptance of everyone with their limitations. One does not approve of the harmful things that others may do, but one accepts them as they are and is ready to help whenever possible—but without trying to change them. One is even content with one's inability to change oneself as one would like while continuing to do what one can to improve, relying more and more upon God and less and less on one's own efforts.

The fifth Fruit of the Spirit is *Faithfulness* (fidelity). Faithfulness is the dynamic expression of meekness. It is the daily oblation of ourselves and all our actions to God out of compassion for others, especially in service of their concrete needs. It serves God without dwelling on what God or others will do for us, and perseveres in giving without thinking of any return. Our normal need for affirmation is coming from a new place: the growing conviction of being loved by God that greatly reduces the desire for human approval.

The sixth Fruit of the Spirit is *Gentleness*. Gentleness is a participation in God's way of doing things that is at once gentle and firm, sustaining all creation with its enormous diversity, yet without effort. We labor in the service of God more than ever, and yet have the sense of stepping back and watching God make things happen according to his will both in ourselves and in others. Our anxious efforts to serve God and our anguished search for God cease. Like God we labor and are at rest at the same time. We work hard but we know by experience, even by bitter experience, that our efforts are not going to go anywhere except insofar as God makes them fruitful. Hence vanity, jealousy, and contention—which often accompany even our spiritual endeavors—are gradually evacuated, leaving immense freedom just to be who we are and to serve the special needs of those around us.

The seventh Fruit of the Spirit is *Goodness*. Goodness is the affirmation of creation as good, together with a sense of oneness with the universe and with everything created. It is the disposition that perceives events, even the tragic things of life, as manifestations of God's love. It recognizes the beauty of all creation in spite of the damage that human selfishness has imposed upon it. As a result, gratitude to God abounds in our hearts and a positive attitude characterizes our relationship with others and with the wear and tear of daily life.

The eighth Fruit of the Spirit is *Long-suffering* (patience). Long-suffering is certitude in God's unwavering fidelity to his promises. Our security is no longer based on anything we might possess or accomplish, but rather on our conviction of God's unfailing protection and readiness to forgive. Hence we are not easily disturbed by the ebb and flow of human events and our emotional reactions to them. Feelings continue to be felt, at times more strongly than ever, but they no longer dominate our awareness or our activity. We are content to wait with confidence for God's deliverance in every situation, especially during prolonged periods of dryness and the dark nights. We have interiorized the words of the Gospel: "Ask and you shall receive. Seek and you shall find. Knock and the door shall be opened to you" (Matt. 7:7).

The ninth Fruit of the Spirit is *Self-control*. Self-control as a fruit of the Spirit is not the domination of our will over our emotions. It is rather our awareness of God's abiding presence and is the result of the infusion of God's steadfast love. Hence our former compulsive reaching out for security, affection and esteem, power and status symbols ceases. In particular, there is no energy for sexual activity apart from commitment and genuine love. When Moses asked God who he was, the answer came: "I AM THAT I AM." This text is still under scholarly investigation, but one likely meaning is "I am *for* you." The inward assurance of God's unwavering love enhances our freedom of choice and action. Out of that interior liberty, self-control arises spontaneously. We know in spite of our weakness that God will give us the strength to get through every trial and temptation. "As the Father has loved me, so I have loved you" (John 15:9).

The Fruits of the Spirit are the new wine of the Gospel that fills us with divine energy and a certain spontaneity. Structures need to be adjusted to this freedom, which, as Paul says, is not license, but an ever-increasing sensitivity to the initiatives of the Spirit. The hallmark of the divine action is, to quote Thomas Merton, "mercy, within mercy, within mercy." The Fruits of the Spirit prove that Christ is living in us and transforming us into witnesses of his continuing presence in the world. To manifest these dispositions of Jesus is the living evidence of his resurrection.

—3—

THE GIFTS OF THE SPIRIT

S T. PAUL SAYS, "IF ANYONE IS IN CHRIST, HE OR she is a new creature" (2 Cor. 5:17). As we dismantle the false-self system, the new self arises with the awakening of the true self. That is the new creation that Paul refers to. The old creation that is passing away is the world of the false self.

The means that the Spirit uses to purify our conscious and unconscious lives are called the Seven Gifts of the Spirit. They are distinguished from the charismatic gifts of prophecy, healing, speaking in tongues, interpretation of tongues, inspired preaching, discernment of spirits, administration, speaking with wisdom and knowledge, and working miracles (1 Cor.12:4–11). These special gifts are designed to encourage the Christian community, but do not themselves transform the person who has such gifts. The Seven Gifts of the Spirit, on the other hand, are acts and movements of the Spirit that purify and raise us to a divine mode of knowledge through the growth of the theological virtues of Faith, Hope, and Charity (Divine Love), which are the transforming virtues in the Christian scheme of things. Isaiah 11:2 lists these gifts as Wisdom and Understanding, Counsel and Fortitude, Knowledge and Fear of the Lord. The Septuagint and Vulgate versions of the Bible add Piety.

The Holy Spirit, through the Gifts, is especially our guide in the practice of Centering Prayer and in accompanying programs to bring its effects into daily life. The presence of the Holy Spirit within us is always inviting us to listen to the delicate inspirations that gradually take over more and more aspects of our lives, and to transform them from expressions of our false self into manifestations of our true self and of the infinite goodness and tenderness of the Father.

The Seven Gifts of the Spirit are intimately connected with the growth of the theological virtue of Charity within us, not only through acts of love of God but also through the way that we relate to other people. As Charity grows stronger, all the Gifts become more and more in evidence. They are like the fingers of a child's hands, which are not capable of much except to reach out and touch your nose. Given a little time and development, however, these same fingers grow and may become capable of incredible skills, such as playing Rachmaninoff on the piano or creating a great piece of art. They become incredible instruments for beauty, goodness, and truth.

So it is with the Seven Gifts. They are infused into our inmost being at the moment of Baptism or the desire for Baptism. We can assume that every genuine seeker of God has them. In the sacrament of Confirmation, the activity of the Gifts is enormously enhanced. Every time we receive the Eucharist, which is a reaffirmation of all that is contained in the sacraments of Baptism and Confirmation, we also receive an increase of the Gifts of the Spirit.

The Seven Gifts of the Spirit are habitual dispositions. A habitual disposition is a way of acting that is permanent, easy, and delightful. The habits infused by the Holy Spirit enable us to enjoy God in some degree and enjoy being like God. The ripe fruits of the Gifts are the Beatitudes, which mean literally, "Oh, how happy you will be," or, as another translation puts it, "Congratulations!"

What are you really doing when you sit down in Centering Prayer and open yourself to God's presence and action within you? You are opening to God's presence and consenting to God's activity. God's activity is the work of the Holy Spirit in your particular embodiment in this world. Jesus refers to the Father's gift of the Spirit in the following passage: "Who among you if your child asks you for a piece of bread would give him or her a stone?" Two thousand years ago in Palestine, bread was designed like flat stones, as is pita bread today. Again, Jesus says: "Which one of your children if he or she asked you for a fish, would give him or her a snake?" Around the Sea of Galilee some fish looked like snakes because they had the shape of eels. Jesus concludes: "If you with your limitations know how to give good things to your children, how much more will the heavenly Father give the Holy Spirit to those who ask Him" (Luke 11:11–13).

There are two ways of asking. One is to put our request into words: "Give me this." Another is to hunger with our entire being, to be a bundle of desperation asking for what we most need or desire. The latter is the basic attitude we assume in Centering Prayer. We are pleading for the supreme gift of the Spirit simply by consenting to God's will and action.

There is another place in the gospels that seems to refer to Centering Prayer in a special way. It is when Jesus said to his disciples in the Sermon on the Mount, "If you want to pray, go into your private room and pray to your Father in secret, and your Father who sees in secret will reward you" (Matt. 6:6). In those days, very few people had any room at all, let alone a private room. Ordinary people lived in one-room houses where the whole family had to make do. Thus we can presume that this passage is meant to be taken metaphorically. When we are told to enter into our private room, we are being invited to enter our inmost being and there pray in secret. Secret from whom and from what, you may ask? Secret from external things, from our thoughts, and from ourselves. St. Anthony the Great is recorded as saying that the only perfect prayer takes place when we do not know that we are praying. Such is the most secret kind of prayer. It brings us into the presence of the Hidden God, the God who is in secret.

Abba Isaac, one of the Desert Fathers and member of a fourth-century lay contemplative movement, has an important commentary on this text, which is quoted in the Ninth Conference of Cassian. Cassian was a Western monk who visited the monasteries of Egypt in the fourth century and later carried their spiritual wisdom to the

West. Much of that wisdom eventually found its way into the Rule of St. Benedict and continues today in Benedictine and Cistercian monasteries, and I might add, in all who practice Centering Prayer. Here is Abba Isaac's commentary:

> We need to be especially careful to follow the Gospel precept which instructs us to go into our private room and shut the door so that we may pray to our Father. And this is how we do it. We pray in our private room whenever we withdraw our hearts completely from the tumult and noise of our thoughts and worries and when secretly and intimately we offer our prayers to the Lord.

In letting go of all our thoughts in Centering Prayer, we follow this advice and enter into our private room. We close the door on our ordinary mental activities such as feelings, images, memories, reflections, as well as perceptions of sensory details from outside such as people and noises in the room or physical things going on inside us. With regard to all the functioning of our ordinary psychological awareness, we simply close the door. In fact, Jesus said, according to some translations, "bolt the door," emphasizing how completely we are to let go of our ordinary level of psychological awareness in order to open ourselves to the spiritual level of our being and to the Divine Indwelling present in secret at the root of our being.

Abba Isaac explains further: "We pray with the door shut when, without opening our mouths and in perfect silence, we offer our petitions to the One who pays no attention to words, but looks hard at our hearts." In other words, God looks at our intention much more than our attention. In Centering Prayer our basic disposition is "Fill me with your Holy Spirit, the supreme Gift, according to your promise. I don't know how to ask rightly, so I sit here waiting, asking you to pray in me, asking for what you most want to bestow, your Holy Spirit."

Finally, Abba Isaac concludes:

> We pray in secret when, in our hearts alone (*not in our imagination, memory, reasoning and sensations*) and in our recollected spirits (*with our intentionality directed to God's presence*), we address God, and reveal our wishes only to Him and in such a way that the hostile powers themselves have no inkling of their nature. (*Italics mine.*)

Our openness to the Spirit might be compared to baby birds opening their beaks for the worm that one of their parents is bringing. Practically half the baby bird is its wide-open mouth. The early monastic Fathers and Mothers believed that if you entertain a thought or image, the demons can tell what you are thinking about and can insinuate just the right kind of temptation to withdraw you from the original purity of your intention. We might also look at it in the light of what we call "the unloading of the unconscious."

Thoughts that emerge from our unconscious as a result of the deep rest of contemplative prayer could easily be interpreted as temptations because of their intense and disturbing character. When they come from repressed memories, emotions arise just as we experienced them in early childhood, so it sometimes feels as if we are being tempted. In fact, we are simply invited by the Spirit to accept the fact of these primitive emotions and to let them go. By coming to consciousness, the feelings' negative energy is released. Hence, we are now more open to the free flow of grace and the positive energies of the unconscious. Until the storehouse of the body is emptied of repressed material and the undigested emotional junk from early childhood, our capacity to respond to the Spirit is limited. When that evacuation occurs through the process of contemplative prayer, our bodies themselves become more cooperative and support the movement of the Seven Gifts of the Holy Spirit within us.

Let us relate the experience of Centering Prayer to the contemplative gifts of the Holy Spirit, which are three: Knowledge, Understanding, and Wisdom. Those who do this practice regularly will notice at times that they have at least two tracks going on simultaneously in their minds. There is the ordinary flow of thoughts passing along the surface of consciousness, somewhat reduced from the ordinary hustle and bustle of daily life, but nonetheless confronting us when we try to be silent. Interior silence is always relative, especially in the beginning. Because we are aware of various thoughts and perceptions going by, we introduce a sacred symbol (e.g., a sacred word) as an expression of our consent to God's presence and action within us. Emotionally charged thoughts are attractive or repulsive and stir up desires or aversions in the unconscious as well as in our habitual ways of reacting to reality.

The three basic instinctual needs of human nature are survival and security, power and control, and affection and esteem. Thoughts or perceptions that appeal to one of those instinctual needs may pull us out of our original consent to God's presence and action within us. It is as if we open the door of our private room and start to come out. When one or more of these instinctual needs has been withheld in early childhood, we tend to repress them into the unconscious or to develop compensatory means of surviving or of reducing the pain of frustration. If we are interested in a big way in security symbols and along comes the thought or image of a nice new car, house, or insurance policy, we may feel a spontaneous interest to reflect on this material. If we consent to the attraction, we are pulled out of our original intention to consent to God's presence. Since the time of prayer isn't over yet, we must begin the process again by shutting the door—and maybe bolting it this time. Then we gently reintroduce the sacred symbol we have chosen to express our original intention.

We need to be prompt but gentle in returning to the sacred symbol whenever we notice we are getting interested in some thought, and especially when we find we are immersed in one of them. We never succumb to self-recrimination. Simply, without attending in any way to what we have been thinking, we return at once to our private room by the gentle movement of the sacred symbol that manifests our intention to be in the presence of God and totally open to God's will.

A friendly attitude toward unwanted thoughts is helpful in order to put up with the constant solicitation going on in our imagination or memory. We have spent a lifetime with unruly habits of thinking and self-reflection, so it will take us a few months, to say the least, to get used to this new way of relating to God, not through our rational faculties, but, as Abba Isaac suggests, by offering God our hearts, the symbol in the Old Testament of our inmost being.

To repeat, it is our hearts that we are offering to God in Centering Prayer, hearts that are pleading for the Holy Spirit and, at the same time, putting up with the weakness of human nature and our own personal melodrama, for the love of God. As we return to the sacred symbol again and again, we gradually become aware that we are cultivating the spiritual level of our awareness. In this sense, every time we move from a thought into the place of interior silence we are renewing our love for God. We do not judge our prayer by how many thoughts we have, however much we are bombarded by them. Rather, we judge it by how promptly we go back *ever so gently* to our sacred symbol. Thus we may have made hundreds of acts of the love of God in the course of a single period of Centering Prayer! The Gifts of the Holy Spirit grow in direct proportion to the depth and sincerity of our love.

We can't go wrong with this practice, except in the following two ways. One is deliberately to engage in some interesting thought, perception, or feeling; the other is to get up and leave. The latter seems to be the favorite response of people who never quite get rooted in this practice. When we are rooted in the practice, we cannot *not* do it. This is precisely one of the signs of the Gift of Knowledge at work in us. We no longer have to find time to do the prayer; the prayer finds us, so to speak. Doing Centering Prayer twice a day becomes second nature. That is the direct work of the Spirit.

An even more certain sign of the work of the Gift of Knowledge arises when, during prayer, along with the thoughts going by and our occasional or even frequent pursuit of them, a third level emerges. This track distinguishes itself from the first two by our awareness of not wanting any thoughts, or, more precisely, of simply being aware that we do not want them. In other words, on the superficial level of consciousness there seems to be an interior built-in detachment from following the thoughts and perceptions going by.

When this awareness is in place, we no longer need the sacred symbol to reaffirm our intention because secretly, as Abba Isaac would say, we are established in our request for the Holy Spirit; we simply want God and nothing else. We are delicately aware of a disinclination for any kind of thought or perception that comes by. Notice I say "disinclination"—not a resistance to some kind of thought (which would be a choice) but the freedom to ignore or disregard all thoughts. This again is a fruit of the Gift of Knowledge that is strengthening our weakness.

The value of being with God during this particular time of prayer is perceived to be so precious that there is no inclination to pursue any thought; or, if there is, one quickly drops it. The Spirit, through the Gift of Knowledge, is gently attracting our spiritual will without our knowing it. We are practicing very subtle but real interior acts that come from the spiritual level of our being.

To sum up, when we experience ordinary thoughts, we gently return to our sacred symbol. But we are also aware at times that God has grasped our will in such a way that we do not want to do anything but stay in his presence. The latter is manifested by an ease in letting go of thoughts or perceptions as they arise.

There is a fourth level in Centering Prayer that you may have experienced. This occurs when you let go of all self-conscious effort to remain in the presence of God and there is little or no self-reflection. On the other levels you may have occasional thoughts like "prayer is going well today" or "I'm very peaceful." In the gift of divine union, the Spirit, through the Gift of Wisdom, grasps our imagination and reflective apparatus and suspends them temporarily, so that we may be filled with the divine presence without any hindrance from our fragile nature and the false self. This is like a kiss. One is totally absorbed in the delight of God's presence. At times there is no reflection of self at all. The wise practitioner of contemplative prayer will not try to prolong this experience, but simply welcome it with gratitude. In this prayer there is no room for pride, because one sees intuitively that only God matters. There is nothing to be proud about. The Spirit initiates us into the reality of who God is—immense, humble, tender, close.

The Gift of Wisdom is communicated in contemplative prayer and brings it to perfection. It is also the source of inspired ministry. We can do the best we can—help other people in different ways—but the Gift of Wisdom enables us to help people in God's way, or to be an instrument through which God directly speaks to people's hearts, always with a view of initiating them into contemplative prayer that opens them more and more to the presence and action of God within them.

The contemplative Gifts of the Spirit are active within us from the moment that we seriously begin to do a regular practice of Centering Prayer. The Spirit then begins to communicate the Gifts of Knowledge, Understanding, and Wisdom. The Gifts are interrelated, as we saw, like the fingers of your hand. Each finger has a special shape and capacity. Each is important and useful, but they all work together. If one grows, they all grow. The contemplative Gifts of the Spirit are God's way of grasping our entire being so that the whole of us may belong to God: body, soul, and spirit.

The active Gifts of the Spirit—Fear of the Lord, Fortitude, Piety, and Counsel—are just as important and necessary. They are designed to enable us to be contemplatives in action, to bring the contemplative experience that we have had in deep prayer into all our activities and indeed in ever greater detail.

Let's take a look now at the effects of Centering Prayer. Obviously the effects are going to be different depending on the tracks that we have experienced during the prayer and how often. To get people started on this journey, we need to encourage them in the beginning to return to their sacred symbol almost continuously; but always gently, always open to the fact that there may be a few moments in which they may be drawn into interior silence. Since our imagination is so habituated to non-stop thinking, it takes a while for the human organism to readjust to a kind of thinking that is simply *aware* of thinking, but without thinking *about* the content's of one's thoughts.

Little by little the influence of the Gift of Understanding manifests itself by introducing us into the Night of Spirit. Spiritual consolations cease and we feel plunged into an abyss of spiritual darkness bordering on feelings of alienation from God. The divine light reveals our bottomless weakness and powerlessness in the face of God's apparent withdrawal. Great doubts regarding faith and trust may arise. The desire to return to moments of union, which we enjoyed in the previous track, causes an acute sense of loss and grief. St. John of the Cross teaches that the pains of the Night are the result of the infusion of divine love, which confronts and dissolves everything in us that is opposed to the love of God. The theological virtues of Faith, Hope, and Charity are liberated from the human props on which they have overly depended.

There is a fifth track of Centering Prayer beyond the level of occasional experiences of union and the anguish of the Night of Spirit. In this fifth track one is totally immersed in the presence or absence of God. This level is the work of the Gift of Understanding and the purification of the unconscious. It is not relational in the sense of conversation or even in the sense of communion, but is a presence in everything we do, even in our thoughts and perceptions during prayer. It is simply the awareness of God experienced but not reflected upon. This awareness is so subtle and so present that it accompanies us into daily life. Until that happens we need to make daily efforts to be constantly reminded of the presence of God.

St. Thérèse of Lisieux taught that to pick up a pin for love can convert a soul. Why not pick up two pins? Or why not have the same loving intention when you brush your teeth, take a walk, have a cup of tea? We can do everything in our daily life with this same intention.

The conviction of being greatly loved by God grows through the Seven Gifts. There is no use moaning because you have too many jobs, too many children, or old folks to take care of. Right where you are, the Spirit's Gift of Piety is suggesting how to transform the situation into a moment of union with God. I don't believe you can do it without a daily practice of contemplative prayer in order to immerse yourself in the reality of the mercy of God's Presence within, which we call the Divine Indwelling. The Divine Indwelling has always been one of the great truths of faith, but it needs to be emphasized over and over again in our day. It is the radical source of the spiritual life. God's pesonal presence is sheer gift. This presence is transmitted to us in Baptism, reinforced in Confirmation, and greatly enhanced in every reception of Holy Communion.

If we emphasize what God is doing for us, as we do in Centering Prayer, we start the spiritual journey from a different place than has been traditional in the past. We begin the journey not with ourselves and what we are going to do for God, but with God and what God is doing for us. We consent to God's presence, letting God decide what he wants us to do. God seems to want to find out what it is like to live human life in us, and each of us is the only person who can ever give him that joy. Hence our dignity is incomparable. We are invited to give God the chance to experience God in our humanity, in our difficulties, in our weaknesses, in our addictions, in our sins. Jesus chose to be part of everyone's life experience, whatever that is, and to raise everyone up to divine union.

—4—

THE GIFT OF REVERENCE

A MONG THE FOUR ACTIVE GIFTS OF THE Spirit, let us look first at the Gift of Reverence. A primary inspiration of this Gift is the realization that our lives are unmanageable and that we will never make headway on the spiritual journey without the grace of God. We are fully aware of our weakness, but also of the unconditional love of God for us, just as we are. God is not judgmental. We are the ones who judge ourselves as we advance in the spiritual journey. The work of contemplative prayer convinces us that we are who we are, and that we are not some idealized image of ourselves that is the result of the emotional programs for happiness or various biases from the culture we happen to belong to.

The Gift of Reverence is also called the Fear of the Lord. The term "fear" does not mean the emotion of fear, but rather fear in the sense of wonder, awe, and reverence. This is the fear of offending God; it is prompted by love and not fear of punishment.

For contemporary Western society, a good description of this gift might be the fear of going against one's own conscience and a genuine respect for ourselves and for our own integrity. This attitude is exemplified in the descriptions of the temptations of Jesus in the desert, where he was confronted with three serious temptations. Jesus responded without fear or panic, stating exactly where he stood. Each time his response put the demon to flight. To be faithful to one's own conscience is characteristic of the Gift of Reverence or Fear of the Lord.

When we follow our own conscience, we manifest our integrity. Whenever we meet an example of integrity in others, we are usually deeply impressed. It is always beautiful, awesome, and inspiring. Jesus manifested this singular integrity in his responses to the temptations of the demon in the desert.

It might be helpful to draw on a contemporary example, even though it is not from real life. The movie

Scent of a Woman, directed by Martin Brest and starring Al Pacino and Chris O'Donnell, is about an old soldier blinded by an accident. He is obviously very angry and close to despair. He decides to have one last fling and then do away with himself. His sister and her husband, with whom he is living, want to take a vacation and they hire a young high school senior in a private boarding school to take care of their brother. The young man sees the three hundred dollars that is offered to take care of the old warrior as a chance to earn the money he needs to go home for Christmas. As soon as the family departs, the old soldier turns up with an elaborate plan to travel to New York. We find out later that he has bought a one-way ticket. Since he is blind, the soldier needs this young man to guide him on the various adventures he has planned before shooting himself. The young man, meanwhile, is in serious trouble because of his refusal to identify one of the other students who did a prank that deeply embarrassed the president of the elite boarding school. The latter tells the young man that, if he doesn't tell who is responsible, he will not be recommended for a prestigious university— thus sabotaging the young man's hopes for the future.

When the grouchy old soldier and the young man arrive in New York, it is obvious that the older man doesn't give a damn about anybody. In their hotel room, the soldier produces a gun and announces that he is going to shoot himself. The young man feels an obligation to do what he said he would do; that is, take care of the blind soldier for the weekend. He demands the gun, but the old man will not give it to him. The old soldier sends him out to buy him a cigar, planning to shoot himself in the boy's absence; but the young man suspects something is fishy and comes back unexpectedly—to the great indignation of the old rascal. The soldier storms that he has no reason to live, and since the student has compromised his own future at the school, they might as well die together. He makes one last offer: "Just leave and I will shoot myself!"

But the young man won't leave. He will not abandon his charge. The old soldier is prepared to push the young man to the very limits of terror. Because he hates himself so much, he does not believe anybody could love him. He challenges the young man to suggest some reason for him to go on living, saying: "I am rotten through and through. I lied to you about not having any bullets left and, if you don't leave, I will shoot you too."

Because the young man refuses to give up on him, the old man is backed into a double bind. He begins to perceive that there may be a reason to live. This makes him so angry that he decides to shoot them both. He grabs the young man by the throat and puts the gun to his head.

"Either leave now or I am going to shoot you!" he shouts. We are focused on the young man's face as he cries out, "Give me the gun! Give me the gun!" He is ready to lay down his life for the old guy, who now backs down. They finally drive home. The young man is still in trouble with the president of the boarding school. Since he has given the old soldier his first experience of real love, the man begins to change. First, we see him defend the young man at the school. Then the children of the family, who have always disliked him, gather around him when he comes home and welcome him instead of running away.

In this story integrity required firmness. The young man did not ask for any reward or thanks. Once the old soldier's basic goodness had been reawakened by the integrity of his young companion in his misadventures, he successfully defended his newfound young friend from the charges that would have ruined his career.

The Gift of Reverence keeps us true to ourselves and to God. It tells the truth in love and will not back down for motives of self-defense or security. Reverence is not only the fear of offending God prompted by love, but it is loyalty to one's own personal integrity: to do what one believes is right no matter what the stakes are. This is the fidelity to conscience that led St. Joan of Arc, at the risk of her life, to stand up to her unjust judges during her ecclesiastical trial. She was burned at the stake as a heretic. Twenty years after her death she was exonerated.

As the Gift of Reverence grows stronger, our trust in God expands. Humility is a profound sense of our weakness and nothingness, but at the same time an even greater trust in God's infinite mercy and compassion. The Gift of Reverence puts together these apparent opposites.

—5—

THE GIFT OF FORTITUDE

THE VIRTUE OF FORTITUDE ENABLES US TO pursue the difficult good on the spiritual journey. The Gift of Fortitude, however, pushes us much further. It gives energy to overcome major obstacles in the way of spiritual growth; it is an enormous reinforcement of the natural and infused virtue of fortitude. The Gift of Fortitude expresses itself in two ways. One is in sustaining people in great ministries that catch the attention of the public. The other is in keeping us faithful to the small duties of daily life in which, for the love of God, we persevere day in and day out in our particular vocation—whether the work be that of a homemaker, grandmother, professional, minister of some kind, or garbage collector. There is a divine way of doing everything. The Spirit shows us how to sanctify our role in life so that we remain in the divine presence. This is why methods of remaining in God's presence are so valuable and necessary if we are seriously pursuing the spiritual journey as an integrated whole.

The instinctual desire for power and control is laid to rest by the Gift of Fortitude, which cannot endure being angry with others. This is not the cringing attitude of passive dependence, however, but rather the unwillingness to put any energy into hostility or anger. The Gift of Fortitude perseveres in seeking the difficult good, even when there is great danger or opposition. The Seven Gifts free us from over-identification with our emotional programs for happiness. When God is present to us all the time, there is no room for fear, because God is the true security.

An eminent example of the exercise of the Gift of Fortitude is the martyrdom of the seven Trappist monks of the monastery of Our Lady of Atlas in Tibhirine, Algeria, in 1996. The monastery had been in Algeria for sixty years, serving as a Christian witness within the Islamic country. After the Algerian government canceled an election in 1991 that it was likely to lose, there was great unrest in the former French colony. Some Islamist groups, who had been likely to win the election, took up arms against the government, and the government in turn took steps to eradicate them. By 1995, the number of dead had risen to 50,000—a number that included at least a hundred foreign nationals as well as several priests and religious. The monks of Our Lady of Atlas, who took no sides in the conflict, decided to stay, even when the situation became very grave. Their leader, Dom Christian de Chergé, stated:

> For this is what I shall be able to do, if God wills: Immerse my gaze in that of the Father to contemplate with him his children of Islam as he sees them, all shining with the glory of Christ, fruit of his Passion, filled with the gift of the Spirit, whose secret joy will always be to establish communion and to refashion the likeness in playing with the differences.

On the night of 26–27 March 1996, men came to the monastery and abducted seven of the monks. Holding the monks hostage, the abductors demanded the release of rebel hostages held by the government. This was not done and, on 23 May, Cardinal Lustiger of Paris extinguished the seven candles he had lit seven weeks earlier as a prayer for the release of the hostages. A week later, the mutilated remains of the seven were found by the side of the road.

The horrified response to the abduction and death of the monks was widespread, with condemnations from Muslims and Christians around the world. Yet what the Algerian martyrs brought about is quite extraordinary. In many parts of the world, especially in Europe, their witness became prominent. It was, and remains, an answer to the enormous questions that arose in the wake of the tragedy of Rwanda, where 80 percent of the citizens were massacred, and where the people doing the killing were Christians—indeed, mostly Roman Catholics.

What the Algerian martyrs have done is to suggest by their lives and martyrdom a new way of being a missionary. They have also pioneered a new way of being monks and nuns in a cloister. Their lives have a significance that vastly transcends their particular time and place. They are exemplars of a new vision of missionary endeavor that involves not so much converting people to Christianity as fostering communion among the people with whom we live, and manifesting respect, understanding, and appreciation of their religion. Such dispositions are the only way to bring to an end the wars and antipathies that have existed between different religions and sacred traditions since history began.

We are now moving into a global culture, a pluralistic world society where grandiose plans for our own particular religious persuasion are either out of date or inappropriate. To this situation, the Algerian martyrs speak with great power. They did not wish to become martyrs. They simply wanted to have dialogue with their impoverished Muslim neighbors, whom they knew were loved by Christ to the point of his laying down his life for their salvation. They wanted to manifest by their own lives the infinite love of Christ for their Muslim neighbors. To do this, they engaged in the study of the Koran with them without any effort at conversion. They supported a clinic—they had a doctor in their community—provided agricultural know-how, and gave generous hospitality to everyone who came to their guesthouse.

For three years prior to their martyrdom they knew they were risking their lives by staying in their monastery. More precisely, they were risking their lives by continuing to serve their Muslim neighbors and living as one of them. The Koran affirms that holy men living in solitude may not be mistreated, but this protection is not extended to those who participate in the ordinary lives of the people among whom they live. The monks thought through, in their own conscience and in the course of many community discussions, what it meant to remain there. Friends and other missionary associates had already been killed by Islamic extremists. The monks knew what they were facing, but they were dedicated to continuing the dialogue of presence to their neighbors, even in the face of imminent persecution. Without intending to, they pioneered a new kind of dialogue that might be called "dialogue unto death." This phrase reflects, it seems to me, the profoundly dialogical character of the Gospels.

The Algerian martyrs refused to judge or condemn anyone: the killers and those who were killed, the oppressors and those who were oppressed. For them, the human family consisted of brothers and sisters—no enemies, not even friends. Their insight was that the world is advancing toward global unification in such a way that the teaching of Jesus—"that all may be one"—is at last coming into full focus. According to Paul, God wills all to be saved. Thus, God must relate as father and mother to every human person.

The biases and mind sets that the monks brought from Europe were gradually dialogued out of them as they met in frequent community discussions and confronted together the increasing possibility of death. But they were not thinking precisely of dying, still less of the glory of martyrdom. They did not want to be the cause of punishment for those who might kill them. The monks in Algeria were preoccupied with plans to improve the quality of their daily lives and monastic witness in little ways: generous hospitality, prompt forgiveness, mutual understanding, and service to their Muslim neighbors. They had heard the word of God in their particular monastic milieu; and they were prepared to live each moment as ordinary monks, no matter what happened. If they were not martyred, all to the good; if they were, they forgave their killers in advance. They were even ready to credit them with a good intention. The monks believed that their vow of stability bound them to the place, not so much a duty as an invitation to unconditional love. In their way, the monks were experiencing the pinnacle of the four freedoms to which the Gospel calls us.

First is the freedom from deliberate sin. Second is the freedom from the roots of sin, which are called, in spiritual theology, the capital sins. Third is the freedom that comes from friendship with Christ, and, still more, from bridal mysticism and conscious union with Christ— the experience of being loved by God and of loving God in return. And, finally, there is simply *freedom*: freedom to be with God in the present moment, whether that involves offering some tiny service, doing the duty of the present moment, or laying down one's life for Christ. As the monks saw it, the choice was all part of the same movement of *listening* to the word of God—at ever deepening levels—and *keeping* it.

Thus, little by little, the Gift of Fortitude, in conjunction with the other Gifts, transmutes the energy of anger designed by nature for defensive purposes into zeal for the service of God and the needs of others. It sustains difficult ministries and welcomes the vicissitudes of daily life instead of fighting or resisting them or giving way to feelings of frustration. It establishes a certain firmness of mind and heart in doing good and enduring evil, especially when these are difficult. It manifests its inspiration in the Beatitude: "Blessed are those who hunger and thirst after justice, for they shall be satisfied" (Matt. 5:6).

—6—

THE GIFT OF PIETY

THE GIFT OF PIETY MELLOWS THE SENSE OF reverence for God and over-strictness with ourselves. It inspires a great spirit of kindness and understanding toward others, meekness in bearing their faults, willingness to forgive, and genuine affection for them.

The Gift of Piety awakens in us a child-like attitude toward God and also a sense that everyone is our brother and sister. It sees people as companions on the journey rather than competitors, even when they have different religious persuasions or no religion at all. The Gift of Piety does not label or put people in boxes. At the same time, it fosters both respect for tradition and creativity in trying to adapt to contemporary culture and the circumstances of daily life.

While the Algerian Trappist martyrs exemplify the Gift of Fortitude, as we saw in the last chapter, the Gift of Piety is equally manifest in them. Let us take another look at the work of grace in these men from the latter perspective.

The monks were living in a Trappist monastery surrounded by destitute Muslim peasants. The monks could have lived inside their cloister with safety, but they felt called to reach out in dialogue and charity to their impoverished brothers and sisters, and to help them as much as they could. Two years before their deaths they had been invaded by guerrillas and ordered to leave, but they simply refused. Through community discussion and sensitivity to their conscience and sense of vocation as monks, they decided to stay—knowing they would probably be killed.

Here is where the Gift of Piety is manifest in them. The monks saw their Muslim neighbors as brothers and sisters, not as enemies or friends. They did not see them as people to convert to Christianity. Rather, they saw themselves as creating community among everyone who lived in that space and manifesting it through sharing their agricultural know-how, as well as cultivating hospitality. By remaining there and maintaining their dialogical relationship with their Muslim neighbors they risked almost certain death; but they were more concerned about improving the quality of their daily lives in the details of monastic life and genuine concern for the local population. They felt that martyrdom was not something to be desired, because they did not want to be the cause of anyone's guilt or punishment. In other words, they were concerned for the salvation of those who might kill them. In their writings we learn that we should pray for oppressors as well as for the oppressed, for those who kill as well as for those who are killed. This is what Father Christian, the leader of the monastic community at Our Lady of Atlas in Algeria, wrote about the possibility of death. He addresses his executioner:

And you, too, my last-minute friend, who would not have know what you were doing; yes, for you too I say this thank-you and this *a-diar* [goodbye]—to commend you to the God in whose face I see yours. And may he grant to us to find each other, happy thieves, in Paradise, if it please God, the Father of us both.

The Gift of Piety enabled the Algerian Trappist martyrs to love even their enemies as brothers and to forgive them in advance for their murder.

This heroic attitude of total forgiveness of everyone and everything is the most mature fruit of the Gift of Piety. As the sense of belonging to the human family as a whole continues to grow through contemplative prayer and practice, this oneness extends to the earth, the environment and, indeed, to all creation. One begins to perceive all things in God and God in all things. The Divine Indwelling perceives Godself in everything that exists.

An example of this new way of seeing reality comes to mind. I often take a walk through a grove of aspen trees on the monastery property where I live. Aspen leaves are extremely sensitive to the slightest breeze. Even when the air is still, a few leaves will always be stirring. Such was the quiet reception I received as I walked into this grove on a certain summer day a few years ago. All of a sudden, a stiff wind came up and rushed through the grove of aspens. All the trees with their leaves sprang unto action. Every leaf was shaking wildly. Branches were bending this way and that, and giving the impression of applause similar to a standing ovation. It seemed as though the aspens were waving at me. Eagerly, I waved back to them, trying in vain to imitate their tumultuous greeting.

But were the aspens really waving to me? Or were they waving to God in me? I waved back to *God in them*! It was a marvelous exchange: God in me greeting God in them. God in me being God in them.

—7—

THE GIFT OF COUNSEL

THE GIFT OF COUNSEL RAISES THE VIRTUE OF prudence to a new dimension. It not only suggests what to do in the long range, but also what to do in the details of our daily lives. The more open we are to the Spirit, the more the Spirit takes over our lives. The Spirit will even live our lives for us. We make many mistakes but keep coming back to the realization that God knows how to live our lives. Only God knows the long road. Only his plans for us are going to work, not ours.

The inspirations of the Gift of Counsel are closer to us than spoken directives. God is so intimately present to us that the constant awareness of God's presence is always available, if we are open to it. It embraces us, everything in our lives, and all reality at the same time. Being in the presence of God as much as we can all day long is the secret of continuous growth in contemplative prayer.

The first thing that emerges as a pattern as we relate to the Spirit as Counselor is the need to change or modify our behavior. The Spirit teaches us how to behave in the Father's house. We are like a youngster brought off the street into a very cultured family that decides to take him in out of charity. He does not know how to behave. When he sees the dining-room table, he puts his muddy shoes on top of it. Someone has to tell him that this is not the way to behave.

I remember hearing a story about a Christian Brother who served in one of the order's homes for delinquent boys. He had a terrible time with one youngster, who was absolutely recalcitrant. For one thing, the boy used to spit in the soup. The Brother tried to persuade him in every way he knew how not to do so, but to no avail. One day, the boy came to him and said: "Guess what, Brother?"

"What?" the brother replied.

"Jesus told me not to spit in the soup."

Thus the Gift of Counsel is not limited to the perfect or well behaved, but engages each of us right where we are, guiding us subtly, but sometimes very bluntly, as to how we are to behave.

The inspirations of the Gift of Counsel are usually practical, concrete, and down to earth— suggesting what to do in practical affairs. They may suggest at times some long-range project. But most of the time they suggest what to do right now and often in great detail, such as what to eat or what not to eat, what journey to take or not to take, when to go to bed and when to get up. The Gift of Counsel may suggest things that seem to be contrary to piety. For instance, it may suggest not entering a form of religious life for which one has a strong attraction. God may see that there will be problems down the line that we do not foresee. The Spirit may recommend something that seems strange, such as taking a job that prevents us from attending mass for weeks or months. The Spirit may give us at the same time a peaceful attraction to accept the position. Later that job may enable us to do great good for others.

The Gift of Counsel is flexible and free of preconceived ideas. That is perhaps what characterizes it as a gift. Practices that we think are essential for our carefully laid plans for holiness tend to get shot through with holes by divine providence.

We need to be sensitive to the divine impulse. The "counseling" is not normally a direct message. It is not a "word of wisdom," which is a charismatic gift in which we are convinced that God is talking to us. The Gift of Counsel is normally a delicate attraction that is peaceful even when it is quite surprising. Everyone who is on the spiritual journey has this gift. Its activity is not the result of our planning or reasoning. In particular incidents, the fact that it was the right thing to do is only revealed somewhere down the road.

A classical example is the sending of the seventy-two disciples to heal the sick and to prepare the way for Jesus to come to various towns. The mission was obviously intended to make an impression, so that when Jesus came he would be well received. The disciples were not prepared for this mission by any standard. They had not been to a seminary. They did not know much scripture. Their nets were scarcely dry on the banks of the lake when Jesus gathered most of them together. These were not the Apostles. They did not have a long experience with him. They were merely a group of men who had been following Jesus for a short time. Jesus said in effect: "Go out now and heal the sick, cast out demons." How would you respond if such a course of action were suggested to you? Jesus sent them out two by two to give them a little mutual support.

But he himself did not go; he sent them off on their own. When they came back, they were full of enthusiasm. The mission was a smashing success. They were excited and thrilled the way people are in a large charismatic gathering with lots of singing in tongues and prophesying.

When the disciples reported their success to Jesus, he told them not to be so excited about their power to work miracles. He put the lid on their enthusiasm, pointing out that they should be more excited about having their names written in heaven—meaning, that they were part of the divine plan. These are words that might be addressed to us. We are part of a plan that we do not know much about. We are trying to follow it and need the guidance of the Holy Spirit through the Gift of Counsel.

Let us take a closer look at the story as it might apply in our own lives. We often find ourselves in a situation where we are given something to do for which we do not feel adequately prepared. Our first reaction is "No." Any decision that is not easy to discern requires that we pray over it. On one level we don't want to do it because we feel totally inadequate. And yet peacefully the thought comes: "Why don't you do this anyway?" The point I want to make is that you may feel that you should go against your better judgment. You feel inadequate and perhaps you are! You feel you may do a lousy job, and so you hesitate.

Three stages frequently occur in action that is prompted by the Spirit. The first is that you feel called by God to do something that requires great effort, and sometimes the project is initially a huge success. The next stage is that your initial success fails. You feel that you made a mistake and are humiliated. You resolve never to take a similar risk. Finally, there is the triumph of grace, often totally unexpected. Those three elements almost always go together. The triumph of grace may consist of the fact that one or two people actually connected with what you were trying to teach, and they then become the nucleus of a tiny group that begins to spread. What you saw in the beginning as success was actually a failure, and what you thought was a failure was really the beginning of a ministry blessed by the Spirit to have far-reaching effects. All you have to do is to take the first step.

In the case of the disciples, as we saw, they were a smashing success. Actually, nothing fails more than success, especially for beginners. Jesus sent the disciples out without preparation, knowing that they would enjoy stunning success and come back with feelings of vanity and pride. That was their failure. He would have to instruct them that *their* idea of success was not what he meant by success. Apparent success, whether it be in ministry or in a vocation suggested by the Spirit, is not what success is. Rather, the humiliation of seeming failure makes certain the triumph of grace. It may not be what you hoped for, but it will be much more successful in the long run than anything you could have imagined.

The Gift of Counsel does not act according to human prudence. What it suggests is not usually a well thought-out plan of action. It might suggest a course that contradicts what has been a great source of support in one's spiritual journey. For example, certain devotions may serve as suitable tools for one period of one's life. Later they may not be so helpful and a new set of tools becomes necessary. This is not to denigrate the great devotions of the Christian tradition. For some people, these may be excellent means all their life. In the case of others, the Spirit may inspire them to drop or add some spiritual practice.

The Gift of Counsel suggests how to adjust to circumstances that are unusual or that change. It may happen that at some point the Spirit will suggest that your sacred symbol is not helpful anymore; it only gets in the way. Or again, you may faithfully say the active prayer sentence and along comes the Spirit saying: "The fruit of the practice has been achieved." When that happens, you do not need the means anymore. It is like taking a train to New York. When you arrive, you do not buy another ticket to go to New York, because you are already there.

This movement into the presence of God in daily life begins by bringing all its details to that presence. What we do as soon as we get up in the morning is important. What we do the last thing before retiring is important. Just what we do may be a question of choice, what works well for us. Some like to read a few lines of scripture before retiring, or as soon as they get up in the morning. Others like to practice Centering Prayer right away. Others say a brief prayer from their hearts as soon as they awaken to give themselves to God. Some people who practice Centering Prayer and who wake up in the night and can't get back to sleep enter into the attitude they have in Centering Prayer; they stay in that attitude for an hour or so and find that it brings them as much rest as being asleep. To be creative about ways to be in the presence of God all day long will greatly enhance our openness to God when we come to Centering Prayer.

The result of many of our practices, including Centering Prayer, is to establish a state in which our spiritual will is constantly turned to God. At some point any specific practice may prove to be a hindrance to the divine action. We may be doing something to help God out when God doesn't need any help. The Gift of Counsel suggests the kind of cooperation we should offer to God, and it suggests when it is no longer useful. Then we should just rest in God. There are people for whom any practice they might initiate would be a distraction. Thus, when something comes up from the unconscious that feels like one of the emotional centers going off, they only have to notice it and it goes away. Any effort to get rid of it would be excessive. When we are at a deep level of peace, even a devout movement is a distraction. It is like the old-fashioned planes that used to fly on a radio beam. If the plane went too far to the right, the pilot heard one beep; if it went too far to the left, the pilot heard two beeps. When there was no sound at all, the plane was right on course and there was nothing to do.

The Gift of Counsel is a peaceful inclination to continue to do what we are doing or to change what we are doing. We can ignore it. It is a suggestion. Take it or leave it. To develop that sensitivity requires work on our part to maintain interior silence, but once it is established the only time we have to take action is when we notice a loss of peace. That means that we are off course. As long as that peace is in place, we are in deep prayer all the time, whether we are praying formally or not. Whether we are counseling or doing heavy manual work, as long as that sense of inner quiet and peace is there, God is not asking us to think about or to judge the situation. He merely wants us to stay on course, to do his will in the present moment. Opposition, negativity, and failure need not be given much attention. Human effort, failure, and the triumph of grace seems to be the pattern the Spirit normally follows. Even that is sometimes hard to perceive because of our preconceived ideas of what the triumph of grace should look like. The triumph of grace is that we accept the humiliation of failure, which is indeed a triumph, a greater triumph than external success.

In actual fact, the experience of failure in ministry teaches us in the long run how to do it, which is *with complete dependence on God.* I do not know whether there is any other way of learning how to do ministry. Failure is part of the learning process. Then, perhaps to our great surprise, everything calms down and works for a while. However, don't count on lingering on that plateau because, just when everything is going smoothly, the Spirit gets a new idea and you are off to the races again!

To witness ordinary people growing in the spiritual journey is a great encouragement. We can see how they are deepening all the time and we wonder how this happens. They all complain about how many failures they are suffering, but in actual fact they are coming closer and closer to God. That is where the real success story lies. They are taking the counsel of the Spirit and putting it into practice.

—8—

THE GIFT OF KNOWLEDGE

THE GIFT OF KNOWLEDGE GIVES US A TRUE idea of the created world in relation to God: it is not a substitute for God, as we tend to make it. The created world is a stepping-stone to God and manifests God. Without that orientation, the created world is sheer vanity or illusion. Since we, too, are created beings, there is a certain humbling character that the Gift of Knowledge imparts—namely that we are basically prone to illusion and that our way of looking at life is not the only way and certainly not the most accurate. Such knowledge opens us, like the opening of mind and heart that we pursue in Centering Prayer, to the reality of God just as God is, without our interpretations—however devout or pious. God is extremely down to earth and has a certain humor and playfulness, qualities that Jesus manifests in the Gospels, especially in the parables.

The Gift of Knowledge is an intuition into the fact that only God can satisfy our deepest longing for happiness. The Gift of Knowledge provides perspective on the energy that we put our emotional programs for happiness that grow up around the instinctual needs of security and survival, power and control, and affection and esteem. While these needs are essential for our survival and growth as infants, they become exaggerated to the degree we feel they have been withheld. Hence, as the compensatory process becomes entrenched, we invest more and more energy in finding in our culture or in our environment the symbols that will satisfy our unbridled needs.

Obviously, given the nature of the false self, we are in competition with everybody else on earth who is trying to do the same unfortunate and childish thing. It can't possibly succeed. When it doesn't work, we are immediately frustrated and so trigger afflictive emotions, such as grief, anger, fear, and discouragement. One's life becomes an endless recycling of desire, frustration, and afflictive emotions. This recycling makes some people so miserable that they opt for some way of ending their pain, such as total withdrawal from life (apathy) or an aggressive program that tries to dominate everybody else. The Spirit of God in response to our Centering Prayer practice provides perspective for the energy that is channeled into this daily frustration of our immoderate desires. The Spirit says to us: "You will never find happiness in any of your instinctual needs. They are only created things, and created things are designed to be stepping-stones to God, and not substitutes for God."

The Spirit presents us with the true source of happiness, which is the experience of God as intimate and always present. Instead of rejoicing with so great a gift, most of us go into a period of mourning. This is natural, because whenever human beings lose something they love greatly, they feel sad. If we think that security, affection, or power are the greatest things on earth and that we are not getting them—or never going to get them—we automatically go into mourning.

In the action of the Gift of Knowledge, the mourning is not like ordinary feelings of grief. It is, rather, constructive and fruitful, because after we get used to the fact that God is the only source of happiness, we have no more energy to invest in these hopeless expectations and so begin to experience peace. The Fruits of the Spirit—Charity, Joy, Peace, and the rest—begin to emerge as habitual dispositions in daily life. The most mature fruits of the Spirit are the Beatitudes, which are even greater dispositions of freedom. Through the exercise of the Fruits, we are not held back anymore by the residue of the emotional programs for happiness that we brought with us from early childhood and that we have been more or less dominated by all our lives.

The Spirit also lays to rest the prejudices and biases that come from the period of age four to eight, when we unquestioningly absorb the values of our culture, parents, education, and ethnic, religious, and peer groups. There is, of course, a certain value in those social entities. It is our over-identification with those values that pulls our energy away from relating to God into various dead ends.

The Gift of Knowledge corresponds to the beatitude of those who mourn. The reason we mourn is that something inside us realizes that our programs for happiness, put together in early childhood, are not going to work anymore. This is one of the intuitive fruits of the Gift of Knowledge. It is the realization of the damage that the emotional programs have done to us throughout our lives up until now. Part of the mourning caused by the Gift of Knowledge is the beautiful grace called "tears of contrition." Such contrition is also known as compunction. Compunction is the humble acknowledgement of our failures without any guilt feelings attached to them. If there are guilt feelings attached to them, then they are coming from our own neuroses. When there is a feeling of loving sorrow for having damaged ourselves and others, these tears are cleansing. Hence the promise contained in the beatitude: "Blessed are those who mourn, for they shall be comforted."

Comfort consists in the exercise of hope. The theological virtue of hope is purified by the Gift of Knowledge and perfects it. Hope as a theological virtue does not depend on the past. In other words, hope is not based on what we have done in the past, whether good or bad. No matter who we are, even if we are the greatest sinner on earth, we can always hope, because hope is not based on past actions. It is based on the infinite goodness and mercy of God here and now—a mercy that never changes.

Those who mourn are blessed because the feeling of sorrow is mitigated and balanced by the theological virtue of hope, as I have just described it. Compunction is a blend or perfect balance of sorrow for real failures and boundless confidence in the mercy of God. Without that balance, mourning turns into discouragement and or even despair. Whenever we feel discouraged, especially when we feel despair over some misdeed in our life, we should immediately remember hope: that God is always waiting for us with unconditional love. The moment that we turn to him with trust in the divine mercy, the past is completely forgotten. God relates to us in the present moment, not in the past or future.

The Gift of Knowledge is the introduction into the Night of Sense, which is the radical placing in perspective of our emotional programs for happiness. It loosens the drive to achieve happiness through the symbols of security and survival, power and control, affection and esteem or through the values we assimilated from our cultural conditioning.

The exercise of Seven Gifts of the Spirit called the Beatitudes are the inner resurrections that take place as a result of the purification and humiliation of the false self. Perhaps the initial Gift that we come in contact with in the practice of Centering Prayer is the Gift of Knowledge, which is the knowledge of creatures in relation to God. This knowledge is precisely what we do not have as we emerge from our childhood with our various ways of coping with traumatic experiences. The Gift of Knowledge impresses upon us intuitively (that is, not through the reasoning process but intuitively as the fruit of prayer) that only God can satisfy. Usually this does not come as a sudden revelation but as a result of the gradual diminishing of our emotional programs for happiness and over-identification with our cultural conditioning.

Our needs for security and survival, affection and esteem, and power and control are stimulated by the symbols of the culture in which we live. When we give ourselves to prayer and submission to God's will, those programs for happiness shift into a new place—to a new building, you might say. But the same tenants remain. In other words, as a consequence of conversion, security comes to mean consolation in prayer; esteem and affection may mean the esteem of our peers, who think that we are holy people; power and control may mean that we have occasional aspirations to be a pastor of a parish, the abbot of a community, or the bishop of a diocese.

Such aspirations are what is meant by "the world" that St. John in his gospel condemns. It is not the world itself that is to be avoided; for the world desperately needs our help. It is our *worldly dispositions* that are the problem— that is, our emotional programs for unlimited security, affection and esteem, and power and control, along with our over-identification with our cultural conditioning.

As we practice Centering Prayer, we begin to get insight into the dynamics of our unconscious. Perhaps through the Enneagram, the Myers-Briggs, or some other self-help program we become aware of our temperamental biases and personality traits. All this valuable information is useful, but it does not go far enough—because temperament and habit are all rooted in the unconscious, and our best efforts on the conscious level can only moderate them. The Spirit comes to our aid to the degree that we sincerely give ourselves to God and make ourselves compliant to the Divine Therapist. Then the unfolding of self-knowledge takes place in which we see the dynamics of the false self interfering and mixing with the motivations of our good deeds.

For instance, we may find ourselves in some worthy ministry while at the same time experiencing some interior uneasiness. In actual fact we may be running away from ourselves or being called by God to greater solitude and silence. Again, we may use our ministry in a workaholic kind of way. Since we are being "workaholics for God," it is hard to discern that our motives are mixed with selfishness and worldliness.

The Spirit comes to our help not to condemn us, but always to encourage us. The Spirit impresses upon us the fact that reality is not the way we see it. We normally see reality through the prism of the desires of our emotional programs for happiness that are rooted in our primitive instinctual needs. Anything that enters the orbit or gravitational field of our basic desires for happiness is judged in terms of whether it serves or does not serve that basic drive or demand. There is nothing wrong with the basic instincts as such. They become distorted or exaggerated in infancy and childhood when these needs are not adequately met.

The Spirit impresses upon us that only God can satisfy our longing for happiness. Notice what this realization does to the false self and to the emotional programs. It tells them in an undeniable way that they are not going to work. If you have spent a significant part of your life with a certain idea of happiness, you will now know interiorly, intuitively, and with certitude that there is no hope of finding happiness there, at least to the degree you had hoped for. What, then, is going to happen to all the programs? They become radically relativized. Now we know they will only bring us a limited amount of satisfaction, not the absolute happiness we had counted on and which turned them into substitutes for God. The net result is that we go through a period of mourning. Whenever you lose anything you love or count on, it is natural to go into a period of mourning.

The Night of Sense usually occurs after enjoying an enriching relationship with God or with Jesus. The scriptures open up for us; we enjoy receiving the Eucharist, spiritual reading, or making retreats. We are attracted to prayer, both private and liturgical. We may even have moments of special consolation or insight. All of a sudden, or gradually, we perceive that our satisfaction in spiritual things was mixed with our emotional programs for happiness. At the same time, the things of God that we once found satisfying become insipid and dull. We grind out rosaries, stations of the cross, visits to the Blessed Sacrament. We dig in our heels and hang on to the pew so we don't leave during Sunday mass. Scripture becomes like reading the telephone book. We feel we are going backwards in the spiritual life. We may even feel that all the good we had experienced is gone forever.

These are some of the signs that the Night of Sense is overtaking us. It is a great mercy of God, because without the relativizing of our emotional programs for happiness, we would go right on looking for happiness under various religious or spiritual disguises. We would be the same old self, only with a new "store front," so to speak—a little more respectable than the one we had before.

The Gift of Knowledge reveals to us that God alone can satisfy and that the pleasures and satisfactions of life are only stepping-stones to happiness. They all have limitations, and to seek to draw from them absolute happiness is not only naive, but just won't work. We have a motive now within us to let go of those emotional programs for happiness, and thus the false self begins to show cracks, and through the cracks come deep self-knowledge and the awareness of the dynamics of our unconscious. We begin to see how these programs interfere with our relationships with other people, with ourselves, and with God.

The Gift of Knowledge is the right ordering of creation in relation to God. It is not a denial of the good things of creation, though it may feel as if we are losing everything. In actual fact, we are gaining the true knowledge of the purpose of creatures, which is to aid and support us in discovering God's presence in everything.

Along with this revelation, which is the major work of the Gift of Knowledge, is the awareness of God in creatures, even in the tiniest of creatures. St. Francis of Assisi offers the most famous example of finding God in everything. It was a gift that Bernie O'Shea also had (see Chapter Eight in my book *Invitation to Love*). Bernie was charmed with daisies, clouds, and indeed, all of nature. He found God everywhere in creation. The Gift of Knowledge enables one to perceive the presence of God even in the humblest of things. It also gives rise to the symbols of the liturgy that are especially meaningful. The symbols of liturgical practice put one in touch with the divine mysteries they contain. It is not in bypassing the symbols, the liturgy, and the rituals, but by going through them that one comes to the mystery to which they are pointing. The Gift of Knowledge suggests persevering in our devotional and liturgical practice and sacramental life during the Night of Sense when, to our natural feelings and senses, they do not seem to be providing any benefit.

The Gift of Knowledge is the first of the contemplative gifts of the Holy Spirit. It initiates the Night of Sense. It is not designed to cause us affliction but to enlighten us by relativizing the emotional programs we thought would bring us happiness. The Night of Sense is painful for *that* reason and not because God is punishing us for our sins. The Spirit of God hastens to assist whatever efforts we make to let go of the emotional programs for happiness.

The Gift of Knowledge also prompts us to let go of our over-identification with our group or roles in life. Examples of this are liberally laid out in the Gospels where we see Jesus acting to undermine the social presuppositions of the people of his time. This was the problem of the Pharisees. They presented themselves as representatives of God when, in actual fact, their observance was worldly and furthering under religious guise the same old programs that people not in religious garb were using to climb the social or political ladders.

—9—

THE GIFT OF UNDERSTANDING
PART ONE

THE GIFT OF UNDERSTANDING IS THE penetration of the truths of faith. This may come during prayer, but is just as likely to come outside the time of prayer. The inspirations of the Gift of Understanding are not ordinary thoughts but rather spiritual impressions or insights that arise spontaneously. Although the time of prayer is not normally the time to think about them, the effect of these inspirations remain with us after the time of prayer. We can then certainly enjoy and relish the penetrating knowledge of the mysteries of faith that they inspire. You may suddenly realize through such an experience what the Communion of Saints means. Or you may get a deeper penetration into the words "The Word was made Flesh." The truths of faith are like the surface of the ocean pointing to the depths, but they do not show us what is underneath the surface, unless the Spirit illumines their deeper meaning. The Gift of Understanding reveals what is hidden in the major truths of Christian doctrine.

The Gift of Understanding perfects, deepens, and illumines faith as to the meaning of revealed truth, adding new depths to the mystery to which we consent. For instance, it could be some aspect of the Holy Trinity or the greatness of God. It could be the presence of Jesus Christ in the Eucharist. It could be the infinite mercy of God in the Sacrament of Reconciliation. In other words, it is not merely the affirmation of something we believe and assent to. A characteristic of the Gift of Understanding is that it provides a kind of living experience of the mystery. One or two of those experiences can last a lifetime and make such a deep impression as to reorient one's whole spiritual life once and for all.

The plank of wood in our own eye to which Jesus refers is a hint that the Gift of Understanding will reveal to us the basic character of our nothingness. This is not a disaster but simply the truth. We are created out of nothing. Given who we are, we have no basis whatever to judge anyone else. The reference to the speck in our neighbor's eye and the beam in our own is a humorous way of inviting us to a deeper understanding of ourselves and enabling us to accept ourselves as we are, whatever that may be.

How does the Gift of Understanding work? Or what are the psychological effects of its direct activity? To answer these questions I will share a personal experience. Perhaps it will jog your memory into some similar experience of your own that enlightened you to the nature of the precious Gift of Understanding and how it enlarges one's perspective of God and the mysteries of faith.

When I was a young man at Yale University I experienced a deep spiritual conversion. I found in the Sterling Library there a set of books on the four Gospels by the Fathers of the Church called the *Catena Aurea*, "The Golden Chain."

Those commentaries opened my eyes once and for all to the fact that the contemplative dimension of the Gospel is the most important aspect of the Christian religion. The Fathers of the Church interpreted the Gospel from that perspective. They called their interpretation the "spiritual sense" or the "allegorical sense" of scripture. There have been different words for this understanding of scripture in different times.

The Second World War was just beginning when I graduated from boarding school. Bombs were falling on Britain and the Blitz was on. Our graduation was overshadowed by the fact that we might not have a future. I had to drop out of Yale because of previous commitments when the course was accelerated because of World War II.

I went to Fordham University for a few months, waiting to be drafted. During the holidays I used to visit the family home on Long Island, and I walked a couple of miles to Mass every day because of the gas shortage. The dear old housekeeper of the local rectory, who was in her eighties, saw this devout young man walking to church and decided he should be in a seminary. She accosted me one day and said, "You must really see the Monsignor. He is very fatherly."

I had no interest in seeing the Monsignor, because I wasn't at all attracted to being a diocesan priest. But I had nothing to lose, so I went to see him, and he did indeed have a fatherly concern for me. He was also a saintly person. He said, "Let me arrange an interview for you with the Bishop."

The Monsignor made the arrangements and I went to see an auxiliary bishop in Brooklyn, who found no difficulty in registering me as a pre-theological student in the diocesan seminary. I received a deferment. As it turned out, my draft number had come up and it was at the very last moment that I received the deferment. Still, I felt uneasy because my friends were all being drafted and some were getting killed. The Monsignor, who himself was dying of cancer, sensed my anxiety and said to me, "*This war is not meant for you.*" For some reason, his words lodged in my heart and gave me a deep peace, in spite of the fact that I seemed to be a draft-dodger to all my relatives, friends, and to myself.

Because I was under twenty-one, I could not enter a monastery without written permission from my parents. They were vigorously opposed to the idea, so I waited until the required date approached and entered the Cistercian monastery in Valley Falls, Rhode Island in January 1944. That was about the time of Anzio Beach and the Italian campaign. I entered the monastery specifically to pray for the soldiers and victims of the war.

I was well aware that I had been spared from this terrible war through no merit of my own. I chose the Trappists because they were the strictest order I could find. In those days it was believed that the more austere way of life you practiced the more likely you were to become a contemplative. I no longer hold that view, but since I strongly held such views at that time, I entered into the full rigors of the life with a willing heart.

Twenty-one years later I was abbot of the monastery and the Second Vatican Council was concluding. Religious orders were called upon to review their rules in the light of the Gospel and modern life. For the first time in 900 years, the observances of the Cistercian order were being reviewed. This was extremely upsetting for many monks. The Trappist life was very austere. We rarely spoke to anyone except the abbot and the novice master. We got up at two o'clock in the morning, engaged in vigorous fasting, heavy manual labor, and long hours chanting the Divine Office in church. We rarely wrote home or received family visits and never went home even for sickness or a funeral in the family. It was a kind of death. My father described it as entering a tomb. He thought that was the end of all the efforts and expense he had put into my education.

With the prospect of a number of profound changes in monastic lifestyle, many cloistered communities were severely polarized. Some monks wanted to be faithful to their original commitments and were profoundly disturbed by any suggestion of change. Others were more liberal and wanted to implement the experiments that were now available to each community. Some abbots at the renewal chapter were like racehorses at the gate, waiting for the signal to take off and implement all the approved experiments. When the permission came, the race was on.

I was in Rome on one occasion with a number of abbots discussing the burning questions of change. They were all more or less distraught. The abbot in a monastery at the time was the man responsible for the final decision in any discussion. Since the monks all wanted different things, it was a no-win situation. There was a sense of frustration, and even desperation, as to what specific choices should be made in the way of experimentation. There also was no time to review issues carefully enough to decide whether it was prudent to change or not. Sometimes life puts one in impossible situations that no novelist could possibly think up. Reality is more unpredictable than any book!

During this meeting, several weary abbots suggested that we take an afternoon off. We drove south and visited Anzio Beach. From there, we stopped at the American cemetery where thousands of American soldiers from the Italian campaign are buried. As I walked into the cemetery with my monastic companions, I looked at the crosses and the stars of David as we made our way down one seemingly endless row of graves. Suddenly I felt as if I was surrounded by friends. It was as if I had come home to a warm welcome among people who greatly loved me. I felt an increasing surge of gratitude that mysteriously surrounded me. I just could not believe what was happening and I tried to conceal my emotions from those who were with me. As I lingered there, I realized unmistakably that these soldiers were my special friends. It was as if they were saying: "Here is the guy who prayed for us when we were going up the Po Valley to be shot to pieces. Thanks for helping us with your austere life and prayers when we desperately needed them."

At that point the words of the Monsignor came back to my mind and I understood in a flash of recognition their profound meaning: *"This war is not meant for you."* The war from which I was mercifully spared did not mean that I did not have a different kind of war waiting for me. It was as if these friends were saying, "You are now in a war that is going to last even longer than ours. We will help you to get through it." I realized I would owe them much more than they ever owed me.

Every now and then a doctrinal formula explodes into experience. I guess the one I received on that occasion was a vivid experience of the Communion of Saints. That doctrine affirms that those whom we have known and tried to serve in this life and who have gone before us are still close to us and are now trying to help us so that we can join them in due time. In any case, everything in human affairs is interconnected. Whatever we do for others now will someday be returned. Even modern physics tells us that, in the physical universe, everything is interconnected. Human beings are one family; we come from one source and are destined for one end. Some are a little further along, and some are falling back and trying again. That experience taught me that everyone is interrelated and that the veil between us and the next life is very thin indeed. That experience gave me the courage to fight the battles assigned to me. Indeed, the war for which God reserved me has lasted a long time. I'm not sure it is over yet.

Words that are casually dropped, as were the words of the Monsignor, but lodge in the heart are called "words of wisdom." They are one of the charismatic gifts described by Paul in I Corinthians 13 and convince you that through them God is communicating something important to you.

Death is only a part of the process of living. If the Communion of Saints has become real for us, then every funeral is a celebration of eternal life. That is the great insight of the Mass of the Resurrection, the new funeral rite. Death is not an occasion only for sorrow, but an occasion of rejoicing that our friends or relatives have moved to a deeper level of union and that we will be with them again. We may not think often of these relationships, but when the chips are down we have lots of friends, and they will never forget us.

The Gift of Understanding may illuminate any of the great truths of faith such as those that we assent to in the Apostles Creed. All of a sudden we penetrate their meaning experientially. Then we know that the Gift of Understanding is working in us and is pushing our faith to new levels of penetration and beyond.

—10—

THE GIFT OF UNDERSTANDING PART TWO

THE GIFT OF UNDERSTANDING CORRESPONDS to the Beatitude of the pure of heart. The Gift of Understanding has two sides: it gives us a penetrating insight into the truths of faith and at the same time a realistic view of our own weakness. When full-blown, it communicates the experience of our nothingness and our incapacity to do anything good by ourselves. The Gift of Understanding is chiefly at work in the Night of Spirit. Whatever interior freedom arises from the purifying love of the Holy Spirit is of immense value and is greater than all external works put together, both for our own redemption and the redemption of the world. We cannot bring this about ourselves, but by submitting to God's purifying love, the Spirit gradually incorporates us into the mystery of the redemption, making us a kind of sacrament of God's presence and a transmitter of divine grace.

The Gift of Understanding is like a laser that casts light into the depths of our spirit and reveals the roots of our emotional programs for happiness as well as all our prejudices and over-identifications with our bodies, feelings, roles, and cultural conditioning. It leaves nothing unrevealed. At first we are not even aware of the hidden tendencies to sin within us: these are sometimes called the capital sins. We may be enjoying the period of close union with God that usually follows the Night of Sense. But at some point God wants us to go to a deeper level of communion, and that involves one of those transition periods on the spiral staircase in which everything is dark. We are disconcerted because we do not know what the next plateau is going to involve.

The insights of the Gift of Understanding bring people into the Night of Spirit. Normally contemplative prayer moves us in this direction. The divine action is thorough and, at the same time, very balanced. In the midst of the awareness of our weakness, or even our sense of rejection by God, there arises an occasional bright spot, a window on the fruits that this purification is bringing about within us. We may enjoy an experience of God that is so delightful that we may think all our troubles are over and we have at last completed the journey. Then after a few hours or days we find ourselves on the spiral staircase again and cannot even remember the pleasures of that transient experience of divine union. The whole purpose of this alternation is to bring the soul to the total transformation of love.

We normally interpret trials as punishments from God. This is a misunderstanding that Jesus tried to clarify. Nothing in this world is a punishment from God but rather a means of healing some hindrance to our entering into the fullness of divine life and love. The Gift of Understanding introduces and sustains us in the Night of Spirit, culminating in the beatitude: "Blessed are the pure of heart for they shall see God" (Matt. 5:8).

At one time, I was at an interreligious workshop in which there was a panel of people who had been through the most barbaric events of our century: two world wars, the Holocaust, Cambodia during the time of Pol Pot, and the Vietnam War,. This was the most extraordinary panel I had ever heard. As each panelist spoke about his or her personal experience, it became more and more impossible to react, because anything one could say would sound like a platitude in the face of what these people had suffered. A Vietnamese girl had been abused by both sides in the war because, as a survivor in her village, she was believed to have cooperated with the enemy; she was threatened with death and raped by both American and North Vietnamese troops. A Cambodian boy was forced to watch the torture and murder that went on twice each day in the camp; yet if he had shown any emotion, he, too, would have been liquidated. He told us that to survive he had learned how never to cry. He had forced himself to show no emotion in the face of such horrors. Now, sensing the immense acceptance and sympathy of this group of people, he actually did break down and weep for the first time.

There was also a Jewish lady on the panel who as a girl had been in the Holocaust. Both her parents were killed in the concentration camp where they had been taken. As she was telling her story, she casually mentioned that she had established a humanitarian organization to prevent things like the Holocaust from happening again. Then, she casually remarked, "I really could not do this humanitarian work unless I was fully convinced that if the situation had been reversed, I could have done the same things that were being done to my people." My ears went straight up as she went on with her presentation. Although she said she had lost her faith in God as a result of losing her family, to me she seemed extraordinarily close to God. She had discovered through terrible human suffering what true humility is. The Night of Spirit brings about the same realization: we know with great clarity that if situations in our lives were changed, we too would be capable of any evil. The fruit of the Night of Spirit is the total turning to God, without reservation and without relying on any form of human support.

The Gift of Understanding, whether it comes through terrible suffering or develops gradually through a life of prayer, makes us aware that we are capable of any evil and that only God is our strength. Only God can protect us from the evil we might do if we were placed in circumstances of enormous tragedy and suffering. In this sharp light there can be no elation or pride in one's own gifts. There is no appropriation of one's own talents. There is no sense of being special or part of an elite. All of this is burned away in the night as we realize ever more profoundly that we owe infinitely more to God and to others than we can ever give back.

Humility is the right relationship to God. It is at the same time total dependence on God and invincible hope in God's infinite mercy. Humble hope is the shortest formula I know for negotiating the spiritual journey.

In the Night of Spirit one goes through periods of intense suffering that can last a long time. In this period, people do not normally benefit from advice but desperately need encouragement. Just to sit with them and hold their hand is much more useful than advice. Advice feels like platitudes to somebody in the state where he or she clearly perceives that all the good things they have received from God are gone, while God seems to have abandoned or rejected them. It is a more intense experience than the Night of Sense, in which sensible consolations are swept away. In the Night of Spirit our relationship with God is questioned on the deepest level and one feels in oneself a kind of monumental corruption. At the same time, as the parable of the Leaven (Matt. 13:33 ff) boldly declares, the Kingdom of God is at work, even in the midst of moral corruption.

An example that might communicate this insight more concretely is something that happened to me while I was going through some heavy trials of this kind. I watched a movie called *Love Story*, starring Ali MacGraw and Ryan O'Neal. It is about a couple who were very much in love— so deeply in love that they literally had nothing but each other. The young man alienated his family, who were well-to-do, by marrying an Italian girl, who had no comparable social background. They married when he was just out of college and didn't have a job. After he got his law degree and a good job, she is diagnosed with cancer and given only a short time to live. They think of taking a last trip to Europe, but she is too sick to travel. In the last scene, she dies in her husband's arms. As the young man leaves the hospital and walks off into the fog, a poignant melody plays in the background. He has lost absolutely everything. His only treasure has been wrenched from him. There is nothing for him to live for. He sits down on a park bench while the fog thickens. We are left with a keen sense of his absolute despair, loneliness, and loss. Sheer loss.

I shed buckets of tears before I realized what this last scene meant to me. It was a paradigm of the way I felt in the Night of Spirit; it was as if God had died and that I had literally nothing left. It was total grief. Having put all my energies into the loving search for God, God seemed to have died or gone away, without even saying goodbye.

It was not the tragic end of the romance in *Love Story* that made it so moving for me, but rather the experience of what it feels like to lose the center of your life. This, I think, is the chief characteristic of the Night of Spirit. There are other pains and much anguish in that Night, but the sense of loss, rejection, and abandonment by God are paramount. People who talk this way may sound as if they need an antidepressant, but that is not the remedy in this case. They need to wait with unlimited confidence for God to complete the work he is doing in secret. He never takes anything from us except to give us something better. When we actually hit bottom and can't go any farther, God will help us. God is not in this to finish us off, but to bring us to Divine Union. The feeling that God is angry with us is a projection of human feelings onto God and is simply not true.

A poem might help to describe the inner dispositions of this state:

The Twilight of Self

My soul is solitary now.
It finds no companionship anywhere—
And no wish to find any.
My sole desire is you,
And you are emptiness and absence
Can one love absence so intensely
That any presence is an intrusion?

I am as one moving in aimless circles.
Rituals, prayers, and sacred symbols
Are meaningless to me.
They communicate nothing of you
Who are eerything to me,
But for whom and from whom I feel no love,
No consolation, and no hope of consolation.

I am as one turned inside out,
And there is nothing there—not you, not me.
There is only your boundless Presence
That treats me like a thing without a heart—
Except perhaps a broken heart.

I long to relate to everyone,
Yet find no way to relate to anyone.
Or is it just a lack of inclination?
For you with whom I desperately long to relate
Are not.

Where now is trust?
Where now is love?
What remains when passive purification is complete
And the Night of Spirit is near its end?
To die to self

Is inner resurrection.
Who I am arises
In the ashes of the self.

—11—
THE GIFT OF WISDOM

THE GIFT OF WISDOM PROVIDES US WITH God's view of things, a kind of divine perspective on reality that penetrates through events and perceives the divine presence and action at work, even in very tragic and painful situations. To see God in suffering is indeed a high level of the Gift of Wisdom. Some things are to be learned in this perspective that cannot be learned in any other way. The Gift of Wisdom is the source of the Beatitude of the Peacemakers, those who have established peace within themselves and who have ordered their own great variety of faculties into a unity that submits to God's direction and inspiration. They are also able to establish peace around them—whether it be in their families, communities, or the workplace.

The word "wisdom" comes from the Latin word "sapientia." The very sound is delicious. "Sapientia" actually means "tasting knowledge"—knowledge that is delightful and not merely notional or abstract. It is like the experience of tasting fruit, a very different experience from reading about it in a dictionary.

Is it really possible to taste God? The answer is yes, but we cannot bring it about by our own efforts. We can only prepare ourselves for it by reducing the obvious obstacles we can perceive and by allowing the action of divine love to purify our unconscious motivation.

The Gift of Wisdom has a very important place in Centering Prayer because it is this gift that causes the prayer at times to be full of insights, delightful, and profoundly silent—a silence that can almost be tasted or heard. The Gift of Wisdom communicates the mystery of God's presence as a personal experience. It brings to an end any doubts about God's love for us that we might have brought with us from early childhood, such as feelings of rejection or lack of self-worth. There is no greater affirmation of our goodness than to be affirmed by the Divine Presence.

Sometimes this sense of God's presence may be personified in one member of the Holy Trinity rather than another working within us. The Abba—which means papa, dad, daddy—was Jesus' favorite word for his experience of the mystery out of which he came.

The experience of God, even in a very modest form, is truly wonderful. I am not referring to the superficial consolation that may come from liturgical music or from some great orator who stirs up our emotions. The stimulation that comes from the senses that stirs up sensible consolation is not the Gift of Wisdom, but is simply a good grace. The Gift of Wisdom comes from a very profound source within and wells up unexpectedly. That is why at times, when Centering Prayer is most dry and we think it is about time to give it up, to our great surprise we suddenly feel completely at peace and virtually caressed by the interior presence of God. Then we wonder what we were complaining about. After all our groaning and moaning, we perceive that God was close to us all the time. Eventually, we grow out of such childishness and become capable of receiving the profound touches of the Divine Presence—not just a drop of heavenly dew, but what seems like waves of love.

One characteristic of the Gift of Wisdom is that it is a permanent gift, even though it manifests itself transiently.

As a permanent gift it shares its inspiration with both the intellect and the will. It is rooted in the will and grows along with charity. Charity grows as a result of acts of mercy and fidelity to prayer. There are serious obstacles to it, such as the unwillingness to forgive and the tendency to bear a grudge or to refuse to be reconciled. These things hinder charity more than other kinds of sins. Divine Love is self-giving, self-surrendering, and very powerful. Contemplative prayer draws us little by little into the stream of charity that flows endlessly between the Persons of the Trinity and through the Incarnation into creation, especially into the human family. Grace keeps inviting us further and deeper into that stream. When you finally lose your foothold in the stream and it carries you along, you are in divine union. Your motive for living and for all activity is rooted in this union.

Once in a while you get a particular insight into the divine. The Gift of Knowledge has to do with human affairs; Wisdom, with things that are divine. Insight into aspects of the divine mystery, such as God's mercy, tenderness, and immensity, are the fruits of the Gift of Wisdom. This affects your conduct so that you begin to be guided, even in daily life, not in detail as in the case of the Gift of Counsel, but from a higher perspective that might be called God's point of view. Seeing things from God's perspective enables us to see all things in God. As St. Thomas Aquinas says in his treatment of this gift, "The gift of wisdom makes the bitter, sweet, and labor, a rest." Even in great tragedy you may find a certain divine sweetness. Somehow, from God's point of view, everything is okay. Everything is in fact perfect. When that higher kind of perspective on reality is missing, we suffer greatly.

When I was about to enter the monastery, I had three or four days at home to say goodbye to my friends and my distraught parents. Nobody in the family had the slightest idea what the Trappists were about. In those days there were only three such monasteries in the United States. I remember walking along the street to visit someone in lower Harlem (where I had been teaching catechism) when I suddenly felt completely surrounded by a marvelous Presence. The sense of being in God was just as powerful on the street as it had ever been in church. I was prepared to go through a wall of fire to enter the monastery. That kind of grace protected me from the poignant goodbyes and gave me the courage to be undeterred by my mother's and grandmother's tears. Neither was a Catholic. My grandmother was especially upset, and there was no way to console her.

At the height of the changes being introduced at St. Joseph's Abbey in Spencer, Massachusetts after the Second

Vatican Council, I had a hernia operation. I suspect that it was due to carrying luggage full of heavy tools to our South American foundations. I was in the infirmary convalescing, and encountering interior trials, as well as dreading some of the experiments in the Trappist regime that I saw were coming. I decided I would take a little walk. As I stepped out of the door of the infirmary onto the blacktop, a Presence of incredible tenderness engulfed me. I happened to look up, and there was a full moon. God showed me in an instant, without words, that he had arranged everything in my life from the beginning to that instant in order to bring me to accept myself just as I was and to give myself to him. Everything in my life fell into place as part of the divine plan. Waves of joy, gratitude, and praise flowed over me from a source deep within. The Presence was so intimate, so penetrating, so respectful of my freedom; so immense and yet humble; so loving and tender; so all-knowing; all powerful and yet so tranquil. It was strength and stability. It was changeless and timeless—it had the fullness of everything. In that moment, I realized that God knew everything about me, even the minutest details of my life, and still loved me! I understood that God had created the full moon *just for me*—just to celebrate this night on which God chose to manifest his love for me. I also sensed in this Presence a certain amusement at my astonishment.

I began walking slowly down the driveway. A large tree next to the road suddenly lit up and my whole life passed in front of my eyes in an instant, leaving the unmistakable impression that everything was okay. I walked into a meadow, where everything was God. The trees, the grass—everything was emerging out of God. I started jumping up and down with joy.

I do not know how much of this grace remained. Special graces are very strong when they first come and then they tend to subside, but the substance of them usually remains. This experience lasted for an hour or two. I kept hopping and leaping around with uncontrollable joy. As I came back to the house, the Presence gradually subsided, and I realized that God created the moon and everything else for each of us, and not just me. With what tenderness and patience God deals with us! There is no word to describe a Presence that is completely unified but which has at the same time such incredible diversity. One cannot exaggerate how good God is or praise him enough. Yet praises are all platitudes compared to the actual sense of the Divine Presence when it finally catches up with you.

It is characteristic of the Gift of Wisdom to show us how God looks at our lives. It is such a total surprise that one cannot get over it. Each person is unique. God keeps bestowing his unconditional love for everyone coming into the world. That is the view that the Gift of Wisdom imparts: everyone is incredibly loved and cared for by God. Even the things we find in our lives to be most destructive are okay, once we turn to God. They are no hindrance as far as God is concerned.

Wisdom is that mysterious quality that cannot exaggerate the goodness of God and that frees us from worldly ideas about God, such as that God is a tyrant who has a hang-up about obedience or a judge ever ready to bring down the verdict of guilty. Or that he is a policeman with a whole KGB of angels watching our every step to catch us in some fault. These are all projections of our fear of the unknown and are most unworthy of God. To inspire us to think big of God, and always bigger, is the work of the Gift of Wisdom. When we need to act out of that understanding, we take on challenges that we would never dare to assume otherwise. The bigger our idea of God, the more likely we are to act with magnanimity in the service of God.

The activity of the Gift of Wisdom establishes peace in us and puts order into all our faculties, relating them to our inmost being where God dwells. This is the peace Jesus speaks of as "not of this world." Once established in this peace, we can be a source of peace to others. Hence the Beatitude: "Blessed are the peace-makers, for they shall be called the children of God" (Matt. 5:9).

The more the Gifts of the Holy Spirit unfold, especially the contemplative gifts of Knowledge, Understanding, and Wisdom, the more one tastes with love and delight the incomparable nature of the Triune God.

Still, the spiritual journey continues even after the movement into Transforming Union. There remains the movement from divine union to unity, the letting go of one's self-identity as a fixed point of reference, a passage that might be called the Night of Self. Perhaps a poem can suggest its extraordinary significance for understanding the purpose and meaning of our lives in particular and the whole process of human evolution.

The Night of Self

When the self relativizes
And the "me" disappears,
There is not much left of time.
There is only the present moment.

Time which once was most of me,
Like "me," is now no more—
Just a memory.

When all anxious seeking stops
Unity begins.
But every time I act
Even if to pray
Unity dissolves.

When all striving ceases
I awaken to behold
Ever-present Awareness
Keeping silent watch.